I0456915

Unspoken

12 Devotions
for What We Carry in Silence

PASTOR JOHN DAVID SMITH

Scribe & Canvas Publishing

South Carolina

Paperback ISBN: 979-8-9995975-1-9
Library of Congress Control Number: 2025943898

Published by Scribe & Canvas Publishing™
Pendleton, SC | www.scribeandcanvas.com

Interior and cover design by Elev8d Designs.
Printed in the United States of America
10 9 8 7 6 5 4 3 2 1

For the ones who smile through the ache,
who keep showing up even when no one sees —
may you finally feel seen.

THE AUTHOR'S VOICE

Dear Reader,

There are some things we carry so long in silence, we begin to believe they don't matter — or worse, that *we* don't matter.

Over the years, I've sat across from people who seemed strong on the outside but were quietly unraveling within. Their burdens weren't always loud or visible. Sometimes it was the weight of unresolved grief. Sometimes, the exhaustion of trying to stay strong. And sometimes, just the ache of being unnoticed in a world that only celebrates resilience.

What I've come to recognize — in my own life and in the lives of others — is that many of us are walking around with stories, wounds, and fears we don't know how to name. Or we've tried to name them, only to be met with blank stares, spiritual clichés, or pressure to "get over it" faster than healing allows.

That's what gave birth to *Unspoken*.

This devotional isn't about answers — it's about naming. It's an invitation to tell the truth — not just to God, but to yourself. To admit the grief you've never voiced, the questions you've silenced, the pressure to perform, the anger that protects your sadness. And through that honesty, to remember: God doesn't wait for us at the end of the healing process. He meets us in the places we're most likely to finally reach for Him.

The moments when we slow down enough to notice Him.

In the middle of the mess — when we finally see that He's been there all along.

May these pages meet you gently.

And may the unspoken finally find a voice.

INTRODUCTION
For the Things We Carry Quietly

This book isn't about answers. It's about naming.

The quiet ache. The silent grief. The pressure to perform. The fear that your pain is too small, too messy, or too much. These are the things we rarely talk about — in church, in prayer, or even with ourselves. And yet they shape so much of how we experience God, healing, and one another.

Unspoken was written as an invitation: Not to perform, but to be present. Not to impress God, but to meet Him. Not to fix everything, but to finally tell the truth.

Each devotion explores a single truth — one unspoken burden at a time. There are twelve, one for each month, but this isn't a race. You're not expected to rush through or follow a schedule. You're invited to breathe, reflect, and wrestle in your own time.

Every devotion includes:
- A **Scripture Anchor** to center your focus
- An **Opening Reflection** to name the quiet tension
- A **Devotional Insight** that explores the struggle
- **Guided Questions** to deepen your reflection
- A **Breath Prayer or Affirmation** to carry with you
- A **Closing Prayer** and **Space** to write what surfaces

This is sacred space. A place to be real, even when that realness is raw. You don't need to be "spiritual enough." You don't have to clean it up before you show up. You just have to begin.

If you've ever whispered, *"Is it just me?"* — this journey was written for you.

TABLE OF CONTENTS

* * *

DEVOTION ONE:
The Loneliest Room in the House

Scripture Anchor

"Turn to me and be gracious to me,
for I am lonely and afflicted."
— *Psalm 25:16 (NIV)*

Opening Reflection

I once stood in a room filled with laughter and still felt completely alone. The room was warm, lit with soft light, echoing with conversation. Glasses clinked. Music hummed beneath the buzz of casual joy. But I, standing among friends and family, felt like a silhouette — like I was there, but not in it. Present in body, absent in spirit.

You know that feeling, don't you?

It's the quiet ache that sneaks in during holidays, or after the kids go to bed, or when no one asks how you're really doing. It's the emptiness that remains after a meeting where you smiled the whole time but said nothing that mattered.

Loneliness doesn't always look like isolation.

Sometimes it wears lipstick and a smile.

Sometimes it sends out birthday invitations.

3

Sometimes it's a mother surrounded by children or a pastor shaking every hand at the door.

Loneliness is not the absence of people.

It's the absence of connection. And that absence is deafening.

Devotional Insight

Loneliness is not a moral failing. It is not a sign of spiritual weakness or poor social skills. It is, in fact, one of the most ancient human experiences. In Genesis, before sin, before shame, there was this divine observation:

"It is not good for man to be alone." *(Genesis 2:18)*

God made us for connection — not just proximity. That's why we can sit next to someone and still feel unknown. Why a house can be full, and our heart still feel empty.

Jesus, too, knew loneliness. He was often misunderstood, misrepresented, and even abandoned. In Gethsemane, his closest friends fell asleep while his soul was in anguish. On the cross, he cried out, "My God, why have you forsaken me?"

Loneliness is not a stranger to God.

And neither are you.

The irony of modern life is that we are constantly "connected," but rarely **known**. We scroll instead of speak. We respond with "I'm fine" when we are unraveling. We mask pain with performance and convince ourselves that strength means silence.

But healing begins with honesty.

If you are lonely, say it.

To God.

To yourself.

To someone who sees you.

Because naming the ache is the first step toward soothing it.

Guided Questions for Reflection

1. When was the last time I felt truly known? What made that moment different?
2. What do I hide behind when I feel alone — busyness, humor, silence, anger?
3. Who in my life might be feeling this same loneliness — and how can I reach them?

Breath Prayer / Affirmation

"I am not forgotten. Even when I feel unseen, I am held."

Closing Prayer

God of the lonely,

You see what others miss. You notice the sigh behind my smile. You catch the tears that never fall. You walk into the room when everyone else has left.

Today, I confess my ache — not to shame myself, but to unburden my soul.

Help me find real connection. Show me where You are already reaching for me — in a kind word, in a quiet moment, in the mirror.

And if there's someone else feeling what I feel, help me be Your presence for them.

Amen.

Your Reflections

Take your time. Be honest. This space is yours.

(Space To Breathe)

* * *

DEVOTION TWO:
The Grief No One Brings Casseroles For

Scripture Anchor

"Blessed are those who mourn,
for they shall be comforted."
— *Matthew 5:4 (NRSV)*

Opening Reflection

There are kinds of grief that never get named out loud.

The loss of a friendship that slowly faded. The miscarriage that no one knew about. The dream that died quietly after too many closed doors. The child that grew distant. The parent who forgot your name.

The love that never arrived. These are the kinds of losses people rarely send sympathy cards for. You won't find them listed in the church bulletin or announced at a memorial service. There's no funeral, no flowers, no eulogy — just an ache that doesn't know where to go.

And because it's invisible, it often gets dismissed — by others, or even by us. We tell ourselves, "It wasn't that big of a deal," or "Other people have it worse." We try to package our pain into something neater, smaller, more acceptable. But the ache remains. Not loud, but steady. Not obvious, but heavy. This is silent grief —

11

the mourning that doesn't make a sound but lingers in the soul like fog after rain.

People around you may not even know you're grieving. You show up. You smile. You keep moving. But inside, you're carrying a casket no one can see. And after a while, you might even forget it's there — until something triggers the sorrow again, and you feel the weight of what was never properly mourned.

Devotional Insight

Grief is not always loud. It is not always public. And it is not always tied to death. Sometimes, it's the subtle unraveling of something you hoped would hold. A "no" when you prayed for a "yes." The slow erosion of joy in a place where you once felt alive.

What makes silent grief so heavy is that it often feels invalid. We compare it to "bigger" losses and convince ourselves to move on. We feel selfish for still being sad, or ashamed that we can't explain it clearly. But God does not grade sorrow. He does not require your pain to meet a threshold before He cares. He does not wait for your tears to be obvious before He offers comfort.

When Jesus said, *"Blessed are those who mourn,"* He didn't include a footnote. He didn't say, "Only if someone else agrees your grief is justified." He simply said: *If you mourn, you are blessed. You are seen. You will be comforted.*

Grief that goes unnamed can still be honored. Sorrow that goes unseen can still be soothed. God is not limited to the visible or the loud. His comfort reaches into the quiet places — where the tears have dried and only fatigue remains… where you're too numb to cry anymore… or where the grief is so deep, you've forgotten what joy used to feel like. Even if no one else sees it — **He does.**
And He does not turn away.

Guided Questions for Reflection

1. What grief have I carried silently because I thought it didn't count?
2. How has that unspoken sorrow shaped the way I love, trust, or hope?
3. What would it mean to grieve openly — with God, or with someone safe?

Breath Prayer / Affirmation

"My sorrow matters — even when it has no name."

Closing Prayer

God who weeps,

You are no stranger to sorrow. You stood at Lazarus' tomb and cried, even knowing resurrection was coming. You understand what it means to lose and still love.

So today, I offer You my silent grief — the one I've buried beneath distractions, shame, or silence.

Hold it for me. Name it with me.

Help me stop pretending I'm fine, and show me that healing begins with honesty.

Comfort me as only You can — gently, patiently, deeply. Amen.

Your Reflections

Take your time. Be honest. This space is yours.

(Space To Breathe)

* * *

DEVOTION THREE:
When Their Blessing Feels Like Your Burden

Scripture Anchor

"Let us not become conceited,
provoking one another, envying one another."
— *Galatians 5:26 (ESV)*

Opening Reflection

You didn't mean to look.

It started with a scroll. A photo. A caption.

Someone just got married.

Bought the house.

Had the baby.

Landed the job.

Took the vacation.

Lost the weight.

Signed the book deal.

And in a split second, without a word spoken, you felt it —
That cold, stinging ache in the chest. You didn't ask for it, but there
it was: the quiet whisper of "Why not me?"

It's hard to admit, but sometimes someone else's joy reminds us
of what we *don't* have. Their highlight reel can feel like a spotlight

on our lack. We say we're happy for them — and we *are*, in part — but underneath, a seed of self-doubt starts to grow.

Comparison doesn't always shout. Sometimes, it sighs.

Sometimes, it disguises itself as motivation or inspiration.

But deep down, it's a wound — an aching belief that we're not enough.

Devotional Insight

We compare ourselves because we crave worth. We want to be seen, affirmed, validated — to know that we matter. And in a world that assigns value based on visibility, achievement, and beauty, it's easy to measure ourselves against what we see in others.

But comparison is a liar. It tells you their success diminishes yours. That their joy makes yours less valid. That there's only so much blessing to go around — and if they got it, you missed it.

But that's not how God works.

The Kingdom of God is not a zero-sum game. It's a feast, not a race. Someone else's abundance is not your famine. Their rising doesn't mean your falling. Their healing doesn't invalidate your pain.

In *John 21*, after Jesus tells Peter what his life will look like, Peter points to John and asks, *"What about him?"*

And Jesus responds, *"What is that to you? You must follow me."*

Jesus doesn't shame Peter — but He does redirect him. He says: *Stay in your lane. Stay close to me.*

Your story is yours. And it is sacred. Even if it's slower. Even if it's quieter. Even if it doesn't look like anyone else's.

There's no need to compete for what God has already promised:

That you are beloved. You are enough.

And you are not behind.

Guided Questions for Reflection

1. Who or what triggers comparison in me — and what does it say about what I long for?
2. What would change if I believed my worth was secure — regardless of what others are doing?
3. How can I celebrate others without diminishing myself?

Breath Prayer / Affirmation

"There is enough. I am enough. God is not late for me."

Closing Prayer

God of immeasurable grace,

You don't rank me. You don't compare me. You simply love me.

Still, I confess: I have measured myself against others — their lives, their joy, their timelines. And I've come up lacking, not because You said so, but because I did.

Free me from the trap of comparison.

Teach me to trust the pace and path You've set for me.

Help me celebrate without envy, and rest in the truth that my life is unfolding exactly as it should.

Amen.

Your Reflections

Take your time. Be honest. This space is yours.

(Space To Breathe)

23

* * *

DEVOTION FOUR:
When You Can't Feel a Thing

Scripture Anchor

"I have become like a man who does not hear,
and in whose mouth is no rebuke."
— Psalm 38:14 (NKJV)

Opening Reflection

There comes a point where the body is too tired to cry, where the soul goes silent from exhaustion, where the heart stops speaking — not because it's healed, but because it no longer knows how to ask for help.

That's what numbness feels like.

It doesn't always look like despair.

It's often more subtle than that.

You still show up. You do what needs to be done. You smile when expected. You answer "I'm good" without thinking. And maybe you believe it. But deep down, there's a hollow place. A quiet ache. A part of you that knows something is... missing. And you don't know when you last truly *felt* something — joy, pain, passion, sorrow. Just silence.

There's a kind of tired that's deeper than exhaustion. A kind of silence that isn't peaceful — just empty. You keep showing up, doing the things, checking the boxes… but inside? Nothing. *It's the kind of fog that settles in without warning — not despair, not peace — just gray.* You're not falling apart. But you're not fully here either. It's like watching your life from the outside, hoping eventually the feeling will return.

Devotional Insight

Emotional numbness is not always the absence of feeling — sometimes, it's the overload of it.

It's the mind's way of protecting itself when the world gets too loud, too painful, too relentless. And rather than letting you break, it quietly turns the dial down. Not to silence, but to static.

You're still functioning. But your spirit? It's frozen.

And in Christian spaces, we don't always talk about this. We praise passion, fire, and "zeal for the Lord" — but what if your soul is tired? What if your prayers feel flat? What if worship feels like mouthing words in the dark?

God isn't afraid of your numbness.

He doesn't shame you for not feeling.

In *Ezekiel 37*, God leads the prophet to a valley of dry bones — lifeless, scattered, long forgotten. And what does God do? He speaks. He breathes. He *calls life back into them.*

You are not too far gone.

You are not too empty to be filled.

You are not too numb to be revived.

But first, you must admit it.

Admit that you're tired. That the fire has gone cold. That the colors have faded. That your soul is whispering instead of singing.

God is not waiting for you to "feel better" before He draws near.

He's already here — in the valley, in the fog, in the numbness.

Guided Questions for Reflection

1. In what areas of my life have I gone emotionally numb — and why?
2. What might I be avoiding, repressing, or overwhelmed by?
3. Where do I sense God inviting me to thaw — even if only a little?

Breath Prayer / Affirmation

*"Even numb, I am not forgotten.
God can breathe life into dry bones."*

Closing Prayer

God of valleys and dry places,

I confess — I don't know how to feel right now. I'm not sad, not angry, not joyful. I'm just… still.

But I know You are not far from this stillness.

You draw near to the hollow spaces. You speak to silence. You resurrect what has gone cold.

I give You what little I have: a whisper of hope, a flicker of faith.

And I ask You — breathe on it. Breathe on *me*.

Amen.

Your Reflections

Take your time. Be honest. This space is yours.

(Space To Breathe)

* * *

Devotion Five:
When Anger Is Easier Than Pain

Scripture Anchor

"Be angry, and do not sin;
do not let the sun go down on your anger,
and give no opportunity to the devil."
— *Ephesians 4:26–27 (ESV)*

Opening Reflection

There's a kind of anger that feels safer than sadness.

It's the kind that builds when you've been hurt too many times — not just by what happened, but by how no one noticed.

It's the heat that rises when your voice was ignored, your boundaries dismissed, your grief misunderstood.

So instead of crying, you clenched your fists.

Instead of breaking down, you built walls.

And somewhere along the way, your pain learned to put on a tougher face — anger.

Because at least when you're angry, you don't feel weak.

At least when you're angry, people might finally listen.

Anger can feel like power. But often, it's just pain in disguise.

Devotional Insight

Anger, in itself, is not a sin.

God gets angry. Jesus turned over temple tables. The prophets thundered with it. Scripture doesn't condemn anger — it *guides* it.

The problem isn't anger.

The problem is what we do with it — or what we use it to cover.

Beneath our rage, there's usually something more tender: fear, betrayal, grief, shame. But tenderness feels vulnerable, and vulnerability can feel unsafe. So we grab the nearest armor we can find — and often, it's anger.

We wear it like a shield: bold, loud, unyielding.

But anger never heals what hurt us. It keeps the pain alive without bringing us any closer to peace. It keeps others at a distance, and God at arm's length.

Yet even in your fury, God doesn't flinch.

He isn't afraid of your anger. He's not put off by your yelling, your silence, or your sarcasm. He sees through the armor and reaches for what's underneath.

Because *He knows what broke you.*

In *John 11,* when Jesus sees Mary weeping for her brother Lazarus, Scripture says He was "deeply moved in spirit and troubled." The Greek suggests a visceral, almost angry grief — Jesus was furious not at Mary, but at the pain death caused. He wept with her. He felt it with her.

God does the same with you.

He doesn't want to steal your anger — He wants to heal your wound.

Guided Questions for Reflection

1. What am I really feeling underneath my anger — grief, fear, rejection?
2. When did I first learn to use anger as protection?
3. What would it take for me to feel safe enough to be vulnerable?

Breath Prayer / Affirmation

"God sees past my anger and reaches for my heart."

Closing Prayer

God who knows my fire,

You see what others don't — the pain beneath my temper, the fear beneath my silence. I'm tired of guarding my wounds with fury. I'm tired of burning bridges just to feel strong.

So today, I hand You my anger — not to be silenced, but to be understood.

Show me what it's hiding.

Heal what it's guarding.

And teach me to feel without fear.

Amen.

Your Reflections

Take your time. Be honest. This space is yours.

(Space To Breathe)

* * *

DEVOTION SIX:
When Rest Feels Like a Risk

Scripture Anchor

*"Come to me, all you who are weary and burdened,
and I will give you rest."*
— Matthew 11:28 (NIV)

Opening Reflection

There's a kind of tiredness that sleep can't fix.

It's the exhaustion that sits in your bones — the kind that shows up after a day full of tasks, when everything is crossed off the list but you still feel empty.

It's the tightness in your chest when you finally sit down and realize you forgot how.

It's the voice that whispers, *"You can't stop now. There's more to do."*

Rest sounds good in theory.

But in practice?

Rest feels like guilt. Like weakness. Like laziness. Like falling behind.

So you push. And perform. And produce.

Because somewhere along the way, you started believing that your worth is tied to your work.

Devotional Insight

We live in a world that glorifies hustle. We celebrate busyness like a badge of honor. We use exhaustion as proof of our commitment. We build lives that never leave room for stillness — and then wonder why our souls are so loud and our spirits so anxious.

But God never designed you to be a machine.

He didn't make you to run without pause.

In *Genesis 2*, before humanity ever sinned, before the fall ever happened, there was rest. On the seventh day, God didn't collapse from fatigue —

He chose to stop. To step back. To bless the pause.

Rest was *holy* before it was necessary.

So why do we resist it? Because rest requires trust.

It means believing the world will keep spinning without us. It means letting go of control. It means saying, "God, I believe You are God — even when I'm not doing."

And that's hard. Especially for the ones who carry everything.

The ones who are depended on. The ones who've been told they must earn their place in the world.

But rest is not a reward. It's a right.

And it's a *command* — not to punish you, but to preserve you.

When Jesus said, *"Come to me, all you who are weary,"* He didn't say *try harder*.

He said *rest*.

Not when it's convenient.

Not when everything is finished.

Now.

Because you matter even when you're not producing.

You are worthy even when you're not busy.

And rest isn't weakness.

It's worship.

44

Guided Questions for Reflection

1. What fears rise up in me when I try to rest?
2. In what ways have I connected my value to my productivity?
3. What would intentional rest look like for me in this season?

Breath Prayer / Affirmation

"I am enough — even when I'm not doing."

Closing Prayer

God of still waters,

I confess that I don't always know how to stop. I've been running so long, I've forgotten what it feels like to be still without guilt. But You didn't create me to burn out. You created me to breathe.

Teach me how to rest — in body, in mind, and in soul.

Help me trust that I'm held, even when I pause. Remind me that rest is not something I have to earn — it's something You freely give.

Amen.

Your Reflections

Take your time. Be honest. This space is yours.

(Space To Breathe)

* * *

DEVOTION SEVEN:
The Ones Who Carry Without Applause

Scripture Anchor

"Carry each other's burdens,
and in this way you will fulfill the law of Christ."
— *Galatians 6:2 (NIV)*

Opening Reflection

Some people don't get to fall apart.

They're the ones who keep everything running — quietly, faithfully, without fanfare. They're the first to show up and the last to leave.

The ones who remember the appointments, refill the prescriptions, wash the clothes, make the meals, say the prayers.

The ones who sit beside hospital beds. Who hold hands in hospice rooms. Who take phone calls at 2 a.m. and never stop saying "I'm here."

Caregivers…

They are nurses and social workers. Pastors and therapists.

Teachers and parents. Adult children tending to aging parents.

Spouses caring for disabled partners.

Friends who never stop being the strong one.

They are everywhere

— and often, no one sees them.

You care. You carry. You hold everything together while holding yourself together. You check in on others. You show up with a meal, a prayer, a quiet presence. You don't expect a standing ovation. But sometimes... it would be nice to be noticed.

Maybe that's you — quietly breaking while holding everything together.

Devotional Insight

Caregiving is sacred work — but it is also costly.

It's holy ground wrapped in exhaustion. A calling that requires everything, and sometimes offers little in return. Many caregivers give from a well that feels bone dry. They serve without sabbath. They smile through the ache. And they rarely — if ever — say, "I need help too." Because if they fall, who will hold everything up?

But even caregivers have limits. Even the strongest need rest. And even those who seem okay on the outside often cry in the quiet corners — not because they're weak, but because they're *weary*. God sees the invisible weight they carry. And He does not expect them to carry it alone.

In *Mark 6*, after the disciples had been preaching, healing, and caring for the crowds, Jesus didn't say, "Keep going." He said, *"Come away by yourselves to a quiet place and get some rest."* He knew their giving had a cost. He honored it. And He invited them to replenish what had been poured out.

If you're a caregiver, this is your reminder:

You are not forgotten. You are not selfish for needing rest.

You are not less faithful for feeling tired. Your care matters. But so do *you*. Jesus carried the cross — but even He needed help along the way. So do you.

Guided Questions for Reflection

1. In what ways have I been a caregiver — physically, emotionally, spiritually?
2. Where am I nearing burnout, and what am I afraid will happen if I stop?
3. Who is helping carry *me* — and if no one is, how can I begin asking?

Breath Prayer / Affirmation

"I carry much — but I am also carried."

Closing Prayer

God of the caretakers,

You see the quiet sacrifices, the late nights, the whispered prayers.

You see the moments no one applauds — and You are moved.

Help me remember that I am more than what I give. That my soul matters too. That You are not only with the ones I serve, but also with *me*.

Lift the weight I've carried too long.

Send help in unexpected ways.

And when I can no longer hold it all together, hold *me*.

Amen.

Your Reflections

Take your time. Be honest. This space is yours.

(Space To Breathe)

* * *

DEVOTION EIGHT:
When "I'm Fine" Is a Lie You Keep Telling

Scripture Anchor

"My grace is sufficient for you,
for my power is made perfect in weakness."
— *2 Corinthians 12:9 (NIV)*

Opening Reflection

You know how to smile on cue.

How to say "I'm fine" in a way that sounds convincing.

How to show up, perform, stay productive, keep moving — even when your soul is screaming for help.

Maybe you've told yourself:

I don't have time to fall apart.

Or worse:

If I unravel, who will still love me?

There's a kind of shame that comes with struggle — especially when you're supposed to be the strong one, the stable one, the spiritual one.

You carry pain in silence, because you've learned the world isn't always gentle with people who bleed in public.

So you hide it. Push it down. Wrap it in performance.

You call it faith, but really it's fear — fear that if you're honest about how *not okay* you are, you'll be judged, rejected, or left behind.

Devotional Insight

Somewhere along the way, we started believing the lie that struggling is failure.

That faith means always being hopeful. That strength means always having it together. But Scripture tells a different story.

In *2 Corinthians 12*, Paul pleads with God to remove what he calls a "thorn in the flesh." Three times, he asks. And three times, God says no — but not because Paul was weak or unfaithful.

Instead, God says: *"My grace is sufficient for you, for My power is made perfect in weakness."*

God doesn't require your perfection.

He doesn't need your mask.

He is not impressed by pretending.

What He wants is your honesty — the kind that says, *"I'm not okay right now… and I trust You with that."*

There is no shame in being human.

No failure in being fragile.

No weakness in asking for help.

You were never meant to carry your pain alone — not from God, and not from the people He's placed in your life to walk beside you.

You don't have to keep lying to protect your image.

The people who love you most won't leave when they see the cracks.

And God?

He already sees them —and calls you beloved anyway.

Guided Questions for Reflection

1. What am I hiding behind my "I'm fine" right now?
2. What keeps me from being honest about my pain — with others, or with God?
3. What would it look like to ask for help without shame?

Breath Prayer / Affirmation

"I don't have to be okay to be loved."

Closing Prayer

God who welcomes my weakness,

You never asked me to be perfect — only present. Yet I've carried this pressure to be okay, even when I'm not. I've hidden my tears behind productivity and my sorrow behind strength.

But You already know.

So today, I stop pretending. I open my hands. I let You see what's real.

Remind me that You are not disappointed. That You do not withdraw when I'm struggling.

Help me rest in the truth that even broken, I am still Yours.

Amen.

Your Reflections

Take your time. Be honest. This space is yours.

(Space To Breathe)

* * *

DEVOTION NINE:
When Letting Go Feels Like Losing

Scripture Anchor

"Trust in the Lord with all your heart and lean not on your own
understanding; in all your ways submit to him
and he will make your paths straight."
— *Proverbs 3:5–6 (NIV)*

Opening Reflection

You plan ahead. You double-check the locks. You triple-check the
calendar. You manage the details, track the numbers, watch the
news, read the fine print. You pray — and still brace for the worst.

Because deep down, you've learned that if you don't hold it all
together, no one else will.

Control doesn't always look like dominance.

Sometimes, it looks like over-preparation.

Like people-pleasing.

Like staying busy enough to never be caught off guard.

Like managing every variable so you don't have to feel
vulnerable.

At its root, control isn't about power — it's about fear.

It's the lie that safety is something we can earn, build, or
schedule.

That if we plan enough, perform enough, please enough, we won't be hurt again.

But control is a heavy god.

And it will never love you back.

Devotional Insight

Scripture calls us to trust God — not because trust is easy, but because it's necessary.

In *Proverbs 3*, the instruction is clear:

Trust in the Lord with all your heart, and lean not on your own understanding.

Because your understanding is limited. Your foresight is flawed. Your logic will not always lead you to peace. But God will.

Still, trust requires surrender — and surrender feels like loss.

We cling to control because it gives the illusion of protection. But the truth is, the more we try to control everything, the less peace we have. Our anxiety grows. Our faith shrinks. We don't pray to commune with God — we pray to get results.

God invites us to lay that burden down.

To release the grip.

To stop orchestrating outcomes.

To step back and say, "Even if it doesn't go the way I want — I will still trust You."

Jesus modeled this surrender in the Garden of Gethsemane. As He faced betrayal, suffering, and death, He prayed: *"Not my will, but Yours be done."*

He didn't pretend the pain wasn't real.

He didn't silence His fear.

But He let go — not out of defeat, but out of divine trust.

And so must we.

Guided Questions for Reflection

1. Where am I holding on too tightly — and why?
2. What am I afraid will happen if I surrender control?
3. What small act of trust can I practice this week?

Breath Prayer / Affirmation

*"I release what I cannot control,
and I trust the One who can."*

Closing Prayer

God of the unknown,

I confess — I like to be in charge. I like to plan, prepare, prevent. But so much of life is outside my hands, and I am tired of pretending I can carry it all.

Help me to let go — not recklessly, but faithfully.

Teach me to trust not just Your outcomes, but Your timing, Your wisdom, Your love.

And when fear rises up again, remind me that You are still in control, even when I am not.

Amen.

Your Reflections

Take your time. Be honest. This space is yours.

(Space To Breathe)

71

* * *

DEVOTION TEN:
When Faith Feels Like a Chore
Instead of a Fire

Scripture Anchor

"How long, Lord? Will you forget me forever?
How long will you hide your face from me?"
— *Psalm 13:1 (NIV)*

Opening Reflection

There are days when prayer feels like reaching into the dark.

When worship feels like habit. When faith — instead of fire — feels more like flicker.

You still believe. But you're tired. Spiritually tired.

You're not walking away from God — but you're no longer running toward Him either.

You used to feel something when you prayed — to hear God in the stillness, cry during worship, find comfort in Scripture.

Now? You go through the motions. You say the right words. You show up, do the devotionals, check the boxes — but the spark feels gone. And you're not even sure when it left.

No one told you that faith could get tired. That belief could feel like burnout. That hope could start to feel like pretending. But here you are — tired of asking. Tired of trusting. Tired of singing songs that no longer stir anything. And yet, you're still here. Still showing up. Still clinging to something you can't quite name.

That quiet kind of perseverance? It matters more than you think.

Devotional Insight

Faith fatigue isn't rebellion. It's not failure.

It's the natural ache of trying to hold on in the dark.

Even David — the man after God's own heart — cried out in exhaustion. *"How long, Lord?"* he asked. *"Will you forget me forever?"* (Psalm 13). That's not a man who's lost his faith — that's a man who's *fighting* for it.

We don't always talk about this part of the spiritual journey — the dry seasons, the doubts that whisper during prayer, the mornings when belief feels more like obligation than joy. But it's real. And it's holy.

Because faith isn't the absence of weariness.

Faith is choosing to stay, even when the feelings fade.

Jesus never promised we'd always feel close. But He promised we'd never be alone. And even when our faith is weak, His faithfulness is not.

Sometimes, worship is loud and full of fire.

Other times, it's quiet — a whisper of *"I'm still here."*

When the prophet Elijah hid in a cave, exhausted and afraid, God didn't come to him in the whirlwind, the earthquake, or the fire. He came in a gentle whisper — a still, small voice (1 Kings 19:11–12). That same voice still speaks to us now — not always in the noise of revival, but in the hush of survival. And both are sacred. So if you're tired, take heart. You're not the only one. And God is not ashamed of your weariness. He meets you in it.

Guided Questions for Reflection

1. When did my faith begin to feel more like effort than connection?
2. What do I miss about my relationship with God — and what might need to shift?
3. How can I give myself grace in this season of spiritual fatigue?

Breath Prayer / Affirmation

"Even when I am tired, God is still with me."

Closing Prayer

God who welcomes my weariness,

You know how long I've been carrying this quiet fatigue — how often I've prayed without passion, worshipped without wonder, served without joy. But I'm still here. And that must count for something.

So I bring You my tired faith. My flickering hope. My dry prayers.

Meet me in the quiet. Revive what's gone cold.

And remind me

that even when I'm too tired to reach for You —

You are already holding me.

Amen.

Your Reflections

Take your time. Be honest. This space is yours.

(Space To Breathe)

DEVOTION ELEVEN:
When Blessings Feel Too Big for Me

Scripture Anchor

"I am unworthy of all the kindness and faithfulness
you have shown your servant."
— *Genesis 32:10 (NIV)*

Opening Reflection

You got the promotion. The scholarship. The clean bill of health. The book deal, the baby, the breakthrough. The promotion came. The opportunity opened. The favor flowed. But something unexpected rose in your chest —

Instead of joy, a strange hush. A tightening. The guilt of receiving what others still lack.

You celebrate quietly. Shrink a little. Smile less. Because part of you wonders… *"Do I even deserve this?"*

People congratulated you, and you smiled — but inside, another voice muttered, *"Why me and not them?"* So you downplayed the win. You shrugged off the praise. You felt almost… guilty.

Success can feel heavy when you know others are still waiting for theirs.

It can feel suspicious when struggle has been your norm.

Sometimes we're more comfortable with scarcity than abundance, because abundance raises questions: *Am I worthy? Will people resent me? Will God take it back?*

So instead of celebrating, we cringe.

Instead of stewardship, we hide.

Instead of gratitude, we apologize.

Devotional Insight

Jacob's prayer in Genesis 32 echoes our own insecurity: *"I am unworthy of all the kindness…"*

Yet God's generosity toward Jacob wasn't a clerical error; it was covenant love.

Blessing is not random lottery. It's gift and responsibility.

Feeling unworthy can be holy if it leads to humility, but it becomes a burden when it silences gratitude or stifles generosity. Jesus' **Parable of the Talents (Matthew 25)** shows servants entrusted with resources "each according to his ability."

The one who buried his gift wasn't humble — he was afraid. Fear turned stewardship into stagnation.

Success isn't meant to cradle ego, nor is it meant to breed shame. It's meant to be **shared**, **enjoyed**, and **multiplied** for good.

Paul captures the balance: *"By the grace of God I am what I am, and His grace to me was not without effect"* (1 Corinthians 15:10). Grace acknowledged and grace activated.

So:

- Celebrate without apology.
- Acknowledge the grace, not just the grind.
- Let blessing become overflow, not dead-end storage.

Gratitude disarms guilt; generosity redeems it.

Guided Questions for Reflection

1. Where have I felt embarrassed or guilty about my own success or blessings? Why?
2. How might I transform my wins into wider blessings for others?
3. What truth about God's character can replace my fear of "undeserved" favor?

Breath Prayer / Affirmation

"Grace given to me is grace meant to flow through me."

Closing Prayer

Giver of every good gift,

I confess the strange knot in my stomach when good things come my way. I worry I'll seem boastful, or that I stole someone else's share.

But You waste nothing and shortchange no one.

Teach me to receive without shrinking, to rejoice without arrogance, to give without fear.

May every success become seed, every blessing become bread, every gift become glory to You.

Amen.

Your Reflections

Take your time. Be honest. This space is yours.

(Space To Breathe)

* * *

Devotion Twelve:
When You Wonder If Your Absence Would Even Be Noticed

Scripture Anchor

"Can a woman forget her nursing child,
or show no compassion for the child of her womb?
Even these may forget, yet I will not forget you."
— *Isaiah 49:15 (NRSV)*

Opening Reflection

You scroll and see celebrations you weren't invited to.

You text and wait for replies that never come.

You post, but no one responds.

You enter a room and feel invisible.

You go through seasons of silence so long, you begin to wonder: *Would anyone notice if I disappeared?*

This is the fear of being forgotten.

It doesn't shout. It whispers. It creeps in during quiet birthdays, empty inboxes, and one-sided friendships.

It grows when the calls stop, when your work goes unnoticed, when grief isolates and joy doesn't bring company.

And perhaps the deepest fear is not just that *people* will forget us —but that *God* will too.

91

Devotional Insight

The fear of being forgotten is ancient.

It lives in the psalms of David: *"How long, O Lord? Will You forget me forever?"* (Psalm 13:1).

It echoes in Job's sorrow: *"You will seek me, but I shall not be."*

It trembles in the voices of prophets and exiles and widows and prisoners.

But Isaiah offers a holy interruption:

"Even if a mother forgets her child, **I will not forget you.** I have engraved you on the palms of my hands." (Isaiah 49:15–16)

God's remembrance is not passive.

It's intimate. Active. Permanent.

He doesn't forget the unseen labor, the unanswered prayer, the night you cried and told no one.

He does not lose track of your life just because the world isn't watching.

Jesus' ministry was full of forgotten people: the woman at the well, the bleeding woman in the crowd, the man exiled in tombs, the thief hanging beside Him.

He not only remembered them — He restored them.

And He does the same for you.

You are *not* overlooked.

You are *not* unseen.

And your presence on this earth *matters* more than you know.

Guided Questions for Reflection

1. When have I felt forgotten, invisible, or unimportant — by people or by God?
2. How has that fear affected the way I see myself or relate to others?
3. What helps me feel seen, known, and remembered — and how can I invite God into that need?

Breath Prayer / Affirmation

"I am engraved in the palms of God's hands. I am not forgotten."

Closing Prayer

God who never forgets,

Even when others move on, even when my voice feels small, even when the silence grows — You remain.

You see what's buried deep. You hold what others overlook.

When I feel invisible, speak my name.

When I feel unseen, draw near.

And when I forget my worth, remind me that I have never once been out of Your mind.

Amen.

Your Reflections

Take your time. Be honest. This space is yours.

(Space To Breathe)

* * *

FINAL REFLECTION
Looking Back, Moving Forward

As you finish this devotional journey, take a moment to pause. What surfaced that surprised you? What silence broke open? Where have you seen God gently draw you closer — even in the unspoken?

Guided Final Questions:

- Which devotion lingered with me the most, and why?
- What unspoken burden do I now feel more willing to face?
- How has my understanding of God, grace, or myself shifted?
- What healing or conversation might I begin because of this journey?

* * *

CLOSING BLESSING
You Are Not Alone

May the parts of you that felt unseen finally feel acknowledged.

May your grief find breath, your weariness find rest, your silence find voice, and your honesty find healing.

May you know, deeply and truly, that you are not alone—not in this valley, not in your questions, not in your quiet.

God is **here**.

And so are we — *the quiet ones* who've whispered the same unspoken prayers...

and now hold space with you in the silence.

ACKNOWLEDGMENTS

To those who've trusted me with your stories, especially the ones that broke open quietly and bravely — thank you. You helped me learn that silence doesn't mean absence, and hidden pain is still holy.

To the friends who reminded me I didn't have to be "okay" to be used by God — your presence healed more than you know.

To the readers who will see their own reflections in these pages— I wrote this for you, and I hope you find language for what you've carried too long in silence.

And to God — who has never flinched at my honesty, never walked away from my questions, and never once forgotten me.

Reader's Guide & Reflection Prompts

Whether you're reading *Unspoken* privately, with a small group, or in a quiet journaling space, the following questions can deepen your engagement:

For Each Devotion:

- What part of this devotion resonated most with my current season of life?
- Did the guided questions open up something I've been avoiding?
- How does this devotion reframe the way I view God in this area?
- What truth do I want to carry into the week ahead?
- Is there someone I can share this reflection with for support or accountability?

Group Discussion Suggestions:

- Open with a short check-in: "Which devotion felt most personal to you this week?"
- Read the Scripture Anchor aloud together.
- Choose one reflection question to focus on as a group.
- Close each session with the devotion's breath prayer or a moment of shared silence.

Want More Space To Breathe?

If these devotions stirred something deep,
and you wish you had more space to process,
write, reflect, or rest…

Unspoken: The Journal
is a guided companion to this book.

It offers extended prompts, space to breathe,
and gentle guidance for the parts of your story
that remain unspoken.

You don't have to rush.
You don't have to carry it all the same way.

There's still room.
There's still time.
There's space for you.

Available wherever books are sold.
Learn more at www.scribeandcanvas.com

Looking for printable tools, group resources, and a free
Companion Packet? Scan the QR code below or visit:
www.scribeandcanvas.com/resources.

www.ingramcontent.com/pod-product-compliance
Lightning Source LLC
Chambersburg PA
CBHW051633120626
46551CB00014B/2057